6. Pray for God's help. You *need* God's help in order to understand what you study in the Bible. PSALM 119:18 would be an appropriate verse for you to take to God in prayer.

7. *Class teachers using this course for group study will find some helpful suggestions on page 95.*

how to
take the self-check tests

Each lesson is concluded with a test designed to help you evaluate what you have learned.

1. Review the lesson carefully in the light of the self-check test questions.

2. If there are any questions in the self-check test you cannot answer, perhaps you have written into your lesson the wrong answer from your Bible. Go over your work carefully to make sure you have filled in the blanks correctly.

3. When you think you are ready to take the self-check test, do so without looking up the answers.

4. Check your answers to the self-check test carefully with the answer key given on page 96.

5. If you have any questions wrong, your answer key will tell you where to find the correct answer in your lesson. Go back and locate the right answers. Learn by your mistakes!

apply
what you have learned
to your own life

In this connection, read carefully JAMES 1:22-25. It is only as you apply your lessons to your own life that you will really grow in grace and increase in the knowledge of God.

1

The Arrival of the King

20th *1:00 —*

MATTHEW 1 AND 2

Introduction to Matthew

Genesis opens with the generations of the heavens, earth and man. Matthew opens with the generations of the God-Man through whom there will be new heavens and a new earth. Sin appears at the outset in Genesis, and its course is traced onward. Salvation is presented at the outset in Matthew, and its marvels are unfolded. In Genesis a nation is founded. In Matthew a Church is predicted and the foundations are laid for it.

Matthew writes especially for the Jews. He uses more Old Testament references than the other Gospels put together. There are 120 quotations from 20 books of the Old Testament. The expression "that it might be fulfilled" occurs many times. Matthew presents Jesus to the Jews as the long-promised Redeemer of the Old Testament. He gives the facts necessary to establish the authority of Jesus with the Jews. His genealogy answers the question every Jew would be asking, "Is He of the house of David?" Matthew deals with His relations to Israel, so he goes back to the head of the race of Israel, to Abraham, and to Israel's great king, David. Luke deals with Jesus as the Son of man and goes back to Adam. John deals with Jesus as the Son of God and goes back into eternity.

Of what practical value, then, is Matthew's Gospel to the Church? It is the bridge between Judaism and Christianity. He presents Christ as the Mediator of a new covenant. There was really no new testament (covenant) until the blood was shed. Matthew shows how evangelical law takes the place of Levitical law; how

2

the high priesthood of Jesus takes the place of the Aaronic; how the temporal promises to Israel give place to the spiritual; how the Passover sacrament gives place to the Lord's Supper; how the Jewish Sabbath gives place to the Christian's resurrection first day.

Matthew shows how the foundations of the Church were laid. Acts and the epistles show us how the superstructure was raised. Matthew therefore goes into greater detail as to the foundation teachings of Jesus, and he is very careful to show that these teachings are meant not merely for the Jew but for the whole world.

Chapter 1 is the Birth Chapter

Matthew traces the ancestry of Jesus back to David, and then to Abraham. As the Son of David, Jesus is connected with the Davidic covenant and the throne rights (II SAMUEL 7:16, 17; I CHRONICLES 17:7-14). This would be the first question to be settled in the mind of a Jew. Is He of the royal line? Is He to be the King of Israel?

As the Son of Abraham, Jesus is connected with the Abrahamic covenant, which has to do with the promised land (GENESIS 12:2, 3; 13:14-17; 15:2-18). This would be the second consideration of a Jew.

It should be noted that while Matthew connects Jesus with the kingly line and proves Him God's appointed King, he nowhere indicates that it was Jesus' purpose in His first advent to overturn the governments of earth and set up His earthly kingdom. This could not occur until the sin question was settled, and the kingly aspect of Jesus' work is therefore always referred to as future, as being the purpose of His second advent.

It will be noted that the genealogy given in Luke (3:23-38) does not correspond with the one given in Matthew. Matthew gives the line from Joseph, the "supposed" father of Jesus, back through Solomon (a younger son of David) to David. Luke gives the line from Mary, the mother of Jesus, through Nathan (another son) back to David. It will be observed, however, that LUKE 3:23 says: "the son of Joseph, which was the son of Heli." The original here merely says "which was of Heli." Since Matthew tells us (1:16) that it was Jacob who begat Joseph, Heli was evidently connected with Joseph in some other way, probably as his father-in-law. Heli seems to have been Mary's father, as an ancient Jewish writing indicates. Further, Matthew and Luke both indicate clearly that Jesus was not the natural son of Joseph. Hence, Jesus, through Mary His mother, was humanly descended from David through Nathan, while Joseph, His foster father, was descended from David through Solomon and the kings of Judah. It is worthy of notice that Jesus is the only person who can prove His descent from David. His genealogies in Matthew and Luke are the only ones from David that have been preserved in the entire world.

1. Who was the real father of the Child Jesus?

MATTHEW 1:20 _Holy Spirit_

2. How should every Jew have known that the Saviour (Emmanuel) would be virgin-born?

MATTHEW 1:22, 23 _prophecy_

The kings of Judah were all descended from David through Solomon, right down to Jehoiachin (also known as Jeconiah, Coniah and Jechonias). Zedekiah followed Jehoiachin, but was the latter's uncle.

3. What curse was pronounced on Coniah?

JEREMIAH 22:28-30 _cut out - no inheritance of the throne_

Many think this curse would have barred Jesus from the throne had He been the natural son of Joseph, who was actually descended from Coniah. Others believe this barrier was merely immediate, not affecting the distant future. It is a fact, however, that Joseph's line is traced through Coniah, and Mary's is not. Jesus was not *begotten* of natural generation. He was born of Mary—not Mary and Joseph. He was not the son of a man. He was THE SON OF MAN, begotten of the Holy Spirit.

4. Of whom was God's Son made?

GALATIANS 4:4 _made of woman_

5. Whose seed was to destroy Satan, according to the earliest prophecy of the Saviour?

GENESIS 3:15 _Eve seed_

4

6. What prophecy, bearing this out, was later given by Isaiah?

ISAIAH 7:14 _God's son Emmanuel_

7. With what special mission was Jesus born into the world?

MATTHEW 1:21 _to save His people from their sins_

8. How did John the Baptist point Jesus out to the first disciples?

JOHN 1:29 _is the Lamb of God_

9. In MATTHEW 1:18-25, how many times at the least, is the virgin birth of Jesus indicated?

MATTHEW 1:18, 18, 20, 23, 25 _5_

10. What had one of the prophets said about Bethlehem centuries before?

MICAH 5:2 _One will go forth from me (B.Y.C.)_

"Bethlehem" means "House of Bread."

11. By what striking name did Jesus refer to Himself in this connection?

JOHN 6:35 _Bread of Life_

12. What wish of David's was fulfilled in Bethlehem?

II SAMUEL 23:15 _thirst quenched as Jesus quenched ours_

13. What is Christ's promise to us?

JOHN 4:14; 7:37, 38 _Living water from Him_

Chapter 2 is the Bethlehem Chapter

The wise men from the East were Gentiles. This seems to be the first indication of the coming fulfillment of God's purposes toward the Gentiles. It is significant that this star was manifested to strangers. Virgil and others say that there was at that time a general expectation of the advent of some great one.

14. What was the twofold purpose of Christ's coming?

LUKE 2:32 _Light to Gentiles, Glory to Jews_

15. To whom was an earlier revelation of the Saviour's birth made?

LUKE 2:8-11 _shepherds_

God spoke to the Jews through an angel, and to the Gentiles through a star—in the language each would best understand, perhaps.

16. What title did the wise men give Jesus?

MATTHEW 2:2 _King of the Jews_

"Born King" is unique. Ordinarily, men are born to be king, or else born and later made king though not born to be.

17. In what spirit did Pilate's soldiers apply the title "King of the Jews" to Jesus?

MATTHEW 27:29 _mockery_

18. How was this title used in the writing above His head on the cross?

MATTHEW 27:37 _Jesus: King of the Jews_

19. How did the wise men use it?

MATTHEW 2:2 (last clause) _reverence_

20. How did Herod and the people of Jerusalem take the news of the birth of the King?

MATTHEW 2:3 _troubled_

This is a summary of today's experience. Christ is either the source of keenest trouble or supreme joy.

There had been recent agitations, so the ancient historian Josephus tells us, and six thousand Pharisees had refused the oath of allegiance to

Herod. They had quoted prophecies of the coming of a King from heaven who would overthrow him. Perhaps this was why Herod was disturbed. Perhaps the people feared Herod's rage. Underneath all this fear was the mistaken notion that Christ's kingdom would then clash with the secular powers. The star itself intimated a heavenly kingdom. The heavenly kingdom was at hand.

21. Who understood Micah's prophecy (Micah 5:2) to refer to the birthplace of Israel's Messiah or Christ?

MATTHEW 2:4-6 _Priests & Scribes_

22. What did Herod pretend he too wanted to do?

MATTHEW 2:8 _To go & worship he Babe_

23. What was the wise men's reaction when they saw the star again?

MATTHEW 2:10 _Rejoicing_

24. In telling of the finding of the right place, does Scripture mention the mother of the Child first?

MATTHEW 2:11 _no "The Child"_

25. When the wise men fell down, whom did they worship?

MATTHEW 2:11 _Jesus_

26. When the angel spoke to Joseph, who was mentioned first?

MATTHEW 2:13 _Child_

27. When the angel spoke to Joseph later in Egypt, who was mentioned first?

MATTHEW 2:20 _Child_

28. Whom does Matthew mention first?

MATTHEW 2:21 _Child_

This is no literary blunder. This Child is God, for God only is to be worshiped.

7

29. What titles are applied to this Child by Isaiah, in one verse?

ISAIAH 9:6 _Child Son, Counselor God Father Prince_

As a man child, Jesus was "born"; as the eternal Son, He was "given," for He was pre-existent.

Here is divine homage paid to an infant in arms, in an obscure house. It is unparalleled. If Jesus was not the divine Son of God, they were gross idolaters. Evidently the Babe Jesus, in all His obscurity, was thought to be greater than Solomon in all his glory, for Solomon was not worshiped.

30. What warning was given the wise men from God?

MATTHEW 2:12 _not to return to Herod_

31. To whom does Matthew apply the prophet's statement about Israel being called out of Egypt?

MATTHEW 2:15; HOSEA 11:1 _after the death of Herod called out of Egypt_

32. What did Herod, in his anger, cause to be done?

MATTHEW 2:16 _killed all males under 2_

Ordinarily, Satan does not seem to be greatly concerned about babies, but how early he tried to kill Jesus! We wonder how God could permit such a slaughter. But remember that these babies were martyrs for Jesus' sake. Surely they will have a martyr's reward. Shall we call them the "infantry" of the army of martyrs?

33. What had God done to the murderer Herod meanwhile?

MATTHEW 2:19, 20 _died_

This is the history of all assaults ever made on Christ and His kingdom —whether by infidels, critics, institutions or nations. They fade away. Those who seek His saving power never die.

34. In what city of Galilee was Jesus reared?

MATTHEW 2:23 _Nazareth_

8

check-up time No. 1

You have concluded your study of chapters 1 and 2, dealing with the Arrival of the King. Review now by rereading the questions and your answers. If you are not sure of some answer, reread the Scripture portion given. Then take the following test to see how well you understand and remember the truths thus far studied.

In the right-hand margin write "True" or "False" after each of the following statements.

1. The angel of the Lord told Joseph that that which was conceived in Mary was of the Holy Ghost. _____

2. The Bible says God's Son was made of a woman. _____

3. John the Baptist pointed out Jesus as "the Light of the world." _____

4. The prophet who said Christ would be born in Bethlehem was Hosea. _____

5. It was David who longed for a drink from the well in Bethlehem. _____

6. The wise men referred to Jesus as "the Son of God." _____

7. The title "King of the Jews" was used above Jesus' cross to indicate the "crime" of which He was accused. _____

8. Herod and the people of Jerusalem were troubled at the report that a King was born. _____

9. The wise men worshiped the Child and His mother. _____

10. The prophet that said "Out of Egypt have I called my son" was Hosea. _____

Turn to page 96 and check your answers.

The Introduction of the King

MATTHEW 3 AND 4

Ten-elevenths of Jesus' life was spent in obscurity at Nazareth. One-third of the four Gospels is devoted to the story of the last seven days of Jesus' life. This is an unparalleled biography. Jesus came into the world to die, not to live. He was now about thirty years old.

Chapter 3 is the Baptism Chapter

1. What did John the Baptist say was at hand?

MATTHEW 3:2 _____

2. What did John say the people must do in preparation for the kingdom?

MATTHEW 3:2 _____

3. What did Jesus say was the great requirement for being a part of this kingdom?

JOHN 3:3, 5, 7 _____

4. Does the fact that one uses religious terms necessarily indicate that he belongs to the heavenly kingdom?

MATTHEW 7:21 _____

5. What did Jesus say in the Sermon on the Mount is perhaps the first requirement? _____

MATTHEW 5:3 _____

10

6. How did Jesus put it on another occasion?

MARK 10:15 _____

Dr. Maclaren says: "The kingdom of heaven is the rule of God through Christ, present wherever wills bow to Him, future as to complete realization." Dr. F. B. Meyer says it is the heavenly kingdom, the reign of God over the hearts and lives of men.

7. Describe the apparel of John, the King's herald.

MATTHEW 3:4 _____

Those who expected Messiah as a temporal prince would look for a forerunner in pomp and splendor. John was unpretentious in the eyes of the world.

8. Did John go to the people or did they come to him?

MATTHEW 3:5 _____

9. In contrast, what does the Lord's Great Commission require of Christians?

MATTHEW 28:19 _____

10. What did John evidently expect the people to do when he baptized them?

MATTHEW 3:6 _____

11. What "washing does every man need?

TITUS 3:5 _____

12. What further significance did the rite of baptism assume after Christ's death and resurrection?

ROMANS 6:3, 4; COLOSSIANS 2:12. Identification with Him in

13. Who besides John discerned the evil motives of the Pharisees and others, and roundly condemned them?

MATTHEW 23:27, 28 _____

Some have said about John: "He is savage, vulgar, sensational." Others have said: "He is a plain talker, but his old axe cut me loose from the world, and he broke my heart with his story about the Lamb of God."

14. Will having good relatives or pious ancestors save anybody?

MATTHEW 3:9; JOHN 8:39, 44 _____

15. What did John say God could do if He wished?

MATTHEW 3:9 _____

16. In what two elements was Jesus to baptize?

MATTHEW 3:11 _____

Baptism with the Holy Spirit evidently refers to believers, while the context indicates baptism with fire refers to judgment on unbelievers.

17. Are all believers baptized with the Holy Spirit into the body of Christ, or only some believers?

I CORINTHIANS 12:12, 13 _____

18. Did John the Baptist discover that Jesus was the One who would baptize with the Holy Spirit and was the Son of God, before or after he baptized Him?

JOHN 1:33, 34 _____

19. Since He was perfectly sinless, why did Jesus insist that John baptize Him?

MATTHEW 3:15 _____

Jesus, evidently, was baptized "unto righteousness" instead of "unto repentance." By accepting John's baptism, He approved John and His message, and began to identify Himself with His sinful people.

20. How many of the three Persons in the Godhead are referred to in connection with Jesus' baptism?

MATTHEW 3:16, 17 _____

21. In what form did the Spirit of God descend upon Jesus?

MATTHEW 3:16 _____

22. What was the Father's estimate of the Lord Jesus at this time?

MATTHEW 3:17 _____

23. Is this same estimate repeated or altered near the end of Christ's ministry?

MATTHEW 17:5 _____

24. If we become sons, or children, of God, how must it come about?

JOHN 1:12 _____

Chapter 4 is the Temptation Chapter

25. Who led the Lord Jesus into the wilderness to be tempted?

MATTHEW 4:1 _by the Spirit_

The word "spirit" is "Spirit" in the Authorized Standard Version.

26. What is Satan's first word in the New Testament?

MATTHEW 4:3 _"If…"_

27. On what occasion was this same Satan-inspired word used again at the end of our Lord's public ministry?

MATTHEW 27:40 _on the cross "If Jesus is the son of God"_

28. What are Satan's first words in the Old Testament?

GENESIS 3:1 _Is that really what God meant?_

13

29. What was the devil's first suggestion to Jesus here?

MATTHEW 4:3 _Change stones into bread because he was hungry_

If Jesus had made stones into bread in this situation, He would have been taking things into His own hands. This is the way many have made shipwreck of God's will for their lives. They doubt God and run ahead of Him.

30. What three words, in the English, spoken here by Jesus form His first "ministerial" utterance?

MATTHEW 4:4 " _It is written_ "

31. What is the best weapon for us to use on the devil?

EPHESIANS 6:17 _Word of God_

The devil's doctrine is that man can live by bread alone.

32. What did the devil try to persuade Jesus to do next?

MATTHEW 4:5, 6 _jump off of the temple_

This is remarkable! The devil was actually showing Jesus how He could manifest a greater faith in the promises of God by trying to force God into a position He never contracted to fill.

33. In quoting the promise, what did Satan omit?

PSALM 91:11, 12 _to guard you in all your will_

34. Whose will did Jesus have to follow to receive protection "in all thy ways"?

HEBREWS 10:7 _to do Thy Will_

35. What does Satan's use of Scripture show about him?

II CORINTHIANS 11:14, 15 _disguises himself_

14

36. When Satan said "It is written" (4:6), what word did Jesus add?

MATTHEW 4:7 _Also ; again_

Some people are afflicted with one passage of Scripture. They take it out of its context and make it support their notions. We need to compare Scripture with Scripture. We need the whole Bible.

37. What did Jesus say God forbids?

MATTHEW 4:7 _Testing God_ (or Tempting)

38. What was Satan's third proposition?

MATTHEW 4:9 _the World for his worship_

39. What did Jesus call the devil elsewhere?

JOHN 12:31 _ruler of this world_

40. What did Paul call him?

II CORINTHIANS 4:4 _the god of this world_

41. From what source will Jesus one day receive the kingdoms of the world?

PSALM 2:7, 8 _from God_

Satan was suggesting a by-pass of the cross to reach the throne. This, to Jesus, was treason.

42. Who later made a similar suggestion to Jesus?

MATTHEW 16:21, 22 _Peter_

43. What reply did He give then?

MATTHEW 16:23 _not to interfere with God's plan " stumbling block; get thee behind me Satan_

15

44. What did He say directly to Satan?

MATTHEW 4:10 _Begone Satan_

Worship + Serve only God

45. To what does Peter exhort us in view of Satan's activity?

I PETER 5:8 _Be alert to Satan + his doings_

46. What is God's guarantee to one who is tempted?

I CORINTHIANS 10:13 _God is faithful, no more than you can beat and away of escape._

When the devil deals with a man who doesn't know his Bible, he has an easy mark. "Thy word have I hid in mine heart, that I might not sin against thee" (PSALM 119:11). This is the best way to carry the Bible. Jesus, in meeting Satan, went directly to revealed truth.

16

check-up time No. 2

You have completed your study of chapters 3 and 4, dealing with the Introduction of the King. Review as before, checking each answer, and if necessary the Scripture portion given. Then take the following test to see how well you understand and remember the truths studied.

In the right-hand margin write "True" or "False" after each of the following statements.

1. John said the people must be baptized in preparation for the kingdom. ___F___

2. John went to centers of population to preach. ___F___

3. When John baptized a person, he expected him to confess his sins. ___T___

4. Paul says in Titus we all need the washing of regeneration. ___T___

5. John said Jesus would baptize with the Holy Spirit and with water. ___F___

6. At the baptism of Jesus, two of the three Persons of the Godhead were referred to. ___F___

7. Matthew says the devil led Jesus into the wilderness to be tempted. ___F___

8. Satan's first word in the New Testament is "if." ___T___

9. Jesus' first "ministerial" utterance was, "Get thee hence, Satan." ___F___

10. In John 12:31, Jesus called the devil "the prince of this world." ___T___

Turn to page 96 and check your answers.

17

A New Joy
Evans

The Principles of the King

MATTHEW 5—7

Chapter 5 is the Beatitude Chapter

Dr. Charles R. Erdman says the Sermon on the Mount is that "perfect standard of conduct by which all men are condemned as sinful and to which they can attain only by divine help."

1. To whom did Jesus commence the Sermon on the Mount?

MATTHEW 5:1, 2 ___Disciples___

2. What is the first requirement for being made partaker of the heavenly kingdom?

MATTHEW 5:3 ___poor in Spirit (meek) humble___

3. Where are the rewards of this kingdom to be given—on earth or in heaven?

MATTHEW 5:12 ___Heaven___

To be poor in spirit is to have a true estimate of oneself, a consciousness of sin and of need.

4. What is the condition for securing the comfort that comes from God?

MATTHEW 5:4 ___those who mourn___

Myrtle Aug 22 Hospital Cataract surgery

5. What is the condition here for coming into a true enjoyment of the blessings of earth?

MATTHEW 5:5 _meek, gentle_

This meekness is the outcome of poverty of spirit and consequent sorrow for sin.

6. Who are the only people who go away from Christ unsatisfied?

MATTHEW 5:6 _those who don't seek righteousness_

7. What serious mistake do some people make?

ROMANS 10:1-3 _not to submit to God's righteousness_

8. If a person expects mercy, what must he do?

MATTHEW 5:7 _be merciful, generous with yourself_

9. What is here made the condition of true spiritual insight?

MATTHEW 5:8 _pure in heart, sincere, transparent her Lord shines through her_

10. What is one great purpose of our redemption?

GALATIANS 1:4; TITUS 2:14 _to deliver us according to God's will, redeem + purify us, to help others_

11. What is good evidence that one is a child of God?

MATTHEW 5:9 _they are peacemakers_

12. How will some treat those who are faithful to Christ?

MATTHEW 5:10-12 _persecute you - bless them_

13. Would the promise of blessing apply to those who are justly criticized?

MATTHEW 5:11 _no_

14. What should make the persecuted Christian rejoice?

MATTHEW 5:12 _pleasing God, reward in Heaven_

19

15. What phrase describes Christians as those whom Jesus intends should preserve the world from going entirely bad?

MATTHEW 5:13 _Salt of the Earth_ /worm /savor (the world)

16. What did Jesus elsewhere call Himself, and here called His disciples?

JOHN 8:12; MATTHEW 5:14 _Light of the World_

17. What did Jesus come to do regarding the law?

MATTHEW 5:17-19 _to fulfill_

18. Under grace, does one depend on the law for justification?

GALATIANS 3:21-24 _No, it does not give life_ _Must have faith_

19. To what three places may rash anger lead one, according to this passage?

MATTHEW 5:22 _Judgement Court, supreme court or council hell fire_

The "judgment" here refers to the local court, "the council" refers to the council of the Sanhedrin, "hell fire" is literally the "Gehenna of fire," figurative of the final condition of the lost. "Raca" was an epithet of intense hatred or contempt, meaning primarily, "to spit." The word "fool" used here means "blockhead" or "idiot," or perhaps "rebel"—a term of condemnation.

20. What should I do in case I have something to give to God and remember that a fellow Christian has something against me?

MATTHEW 5:23, 24 _be reconciled first_

21. Where does adultery begin, in the sight of God?

PROVERBS 6:25; MATTHEW 5:28 _in his eyes_

22. When lust or desire has been conceived in the heart, what often happens?

JAMES 1:14, 15 _Sin leading to death_

23. What does Paul say must be done with the affections and lusts that destroy spiritual life?

GALATIANS 5:24 _Crucify the flesh_
"death"

24. Is marriage a human or a divine institution?

GENESIS 2:23, 24 _divine_

25. In the sight of God, can the marriage tie be severed by man?

MATTHEW 19:6 _No_

26. Does Jesus' own action seem to indicate we are to take His words about turning the other cheek literally or in principle?

MATTHEW 5:39; JOHN 18:22, 23 _literally_
as Christ did

27. In dealing with others, even enemies, what one word describes the emotion that should possess us?

MATTHEW 5:44 _forgiving; love them + pray for them_

28. What should be the ultimate objective of every Christian?

MATTHEW 5:48 _be like Jesus; perfect;_
His Total Will - daily love

Chapter 6 is the Prayer Chapter

29. What did Jesus warn us against in doing our good deeds?

MATTHEW 6:1 _pride; to be noticed; to impress men_

30. In what spirit should we always do our good deeds, if we would earn a reward?

I CORINTHIANS 13:3 _in love_

31. When a person does his good deeds for publicity, when does he get his sole reward?

MATTHEW 6:2 _on earth_

32. When a person does good deeds with the proper motive, what will he eventually receive?

MATTHEW 6:20 _rewards in Heaven_

33. What did Jesus say regarding our manner of giving?

MATTHEW 6:3 _give without others knowing_

The thought here seems to be that so far as possible we should dismiss the deed from our own consciousness.

34. Who is always observing when we do good?

MATTHEW 6:4 _God_

Perhaps the worst form of pride is the desire to appear humble. Some even pray to exhibit their piety.

35. What is a person's sole reward if he prays for the purpose of exhibition?

MATTHEW 6:5 _being seen by men_

36. How did Jesus express the idea of praying in strict privacy?

MATTHEW 6:6 _go into your inner room_

37. What kind of repetition in prayer did Jesus condemn?

MATTHEW 6:7 _meaningless repetition before others_

38. Even though God knows all our needs beforehand, what does He direct us to do?

PHILIPPIANS 4:6 _In all things by prayer let your requests be made known to God_

Prayer is not for the purpose of informing or persuading God; nor is it to try to conform God's will to ours, but our will to His.

39. To whom alone belongs the privilege of calling God "Father"?

GALATIANS 4:6 _His children_

The Lord gave this prayer to His disciples as a pattern. It is a prayer for the children of God—"our Father."

40. After becoming children of God through faith in Christ, and receiving His forgiveness so far as eternity is concerned, what must we do if we expect to be forgiven the wrongs we do within the family?

MATTHEW 6:12 _forgive others_

Judicial forgiveness for eternity is dependent, not on our forgiving others, but on our trusting Christ for His salvation (JOHN 6:47). This trusting, and the salvation it brings, should lead us to forgive others.

41. Does God ever tempt any man to sin?

JAMES 1:13 _no_

42. If we want to be led out of temptation, or enabled to bear it, what must we look for?

I CORINTHIANS 10:13 _the way God provides for escape_

43. What puts believers under great obligation to forgive others?

EPHESIANS 4:32 _God in Christ forgave us_

44. Why is the amassing of riches vain?

PSALM 39:6 _does not know who will gather them_

45. What does James indicate is true riches?

JAMES 2:5 _rich in faith + heirs of Kingdom_

46. Does our treasure follow our heart, or our heart our treasure?

MATTHEW 6:21 _____

Evil affections obscure the sight of conscience and leave one in darkness.

47. How did Jesus state the impossibility of serving God in part and money or gain in part?

MATTHEW 6:24 _No man can serve two Masters_

48. Why is it ruinous to love money?

I Timothy 6:9, 10 _fall into temptation, root of evil_

In Matthew 6:25, "Take no thought" is "Be not anxious" in A.S.V.

49. What should believers do with their burdens?

Psalm 55:22; I Peter 5:7 _cast upon Lord_

50. In how many matters should we be anxious?

Philippians 4:6, 7 _for nothing_

"Be careful for nothing" is "In nothing be anxious," in A.S.V.

51. If we put God first, what will He do regarding our temporal needs?

Matthew 6:33 _all you need will be added to you_

Chapter 7 is the Judging Chapter

52. Why is it risky for us to judge others?

Matthew 7:1 _you will be judged as you judge_

53. Was Jesus here warning against forming opinions regarding obvious facts or regarding people's motives?

Matthew 7:6, 16 _____

54. If a person is always seeking to get the better of someone, what may he expect of his fellow men?

Matthew 7:2 _expect what you give_

55. What did Jesus say is an unsafe way to judge?

John 7:24 _according to appearance_

56. What does Paul say about judging others when blind to our own faults?

Romans 2:21-23 _do what we teach & preach_

There are occasions when judging, or weighing evidence, is necessary.

57. How may a person expect to be evaluated if he is pulling motes out of others' eyes while having a beam in his own eye?

Matthew 7:5 _as a hypocrite_

58. Using the first letter of the first word in each clause in verse 7, what do you get?

Matthew 7:7 _a asa ka ask seek & knock_

59. What is a basic condition of prevailing prayer?

Psalm 66:18 _no wickedness in heart_

60. When shall we really reach God in prayer?

Jeremiah 29:12, 13 _when we seek with all our heart_

61. What sort of gifts will God always give His children?

Matthew 7:11 _what is good_

62. If a man wants life, what way must he take?

Matthew 7:13, 14 _the narrow way_

63. What is one of the surest ways to detect a false prophet or leader?

Matthew 7:16 _by his fruits_

64. Who is never deceived by smooth but false claims?

Matthew 7:23 _God_

65. What two kinds of people hear or read the words of Jesus?

Matthew 7:24, 26 _wise   foolish_

check-up time No. 3

You have finished your study of chapters 5–7, dealing with the Principles of the King. Review as formerly, checking each answer, and if necessary the Scripture portion given. Then take the following test to see how well you understand and remember the truths studied.

In the right-hand margin write "True" or "False" after each of the following statements.

1. Jesus began the Sermon on the Mount to His disciples. _____ T

2. True spiritual insight is given to the meek. _____ F

3. Jesus called His disciples the light of the world. _____ T

4. Marriage is a divine institution. _____ T

5. Jesus condemned all repetition in prayer. _____ F

6. The prayer Jesus taught His disciples in Matthew 6 is for believers only. _____ T

7. It is impossible to serve both God and riches. _____ T

8. Jesus says we must never judge others. _____ F

9. A person who pulls motes out of others' eyes when he has a beam in his own is a hypocrite. _____ T

10. The two kinds of people who read Jesus' words are the good and the bad. _____ F

Turn to page 96 and check your answers.

The Credentials of the King

MATTHEW 8—10

Chapter 8 is the Healing Chapter

Jesus' sayings in chapters 5—7 are followed by His deeds here.

1. What was the great purpose of Jesus' miracles?

MATTHEW 9:6; ACTS 2:22 _____

2. Why were miraculous powers also delegated to the apostles?

II CORINTHIANS 12:12; HEBREWS 2:3, 4 _____

3. Did the leper question Jesus' ability or His willingness?

MATTHEW 8:2 _____

4. How did the centurion expect his servant to be healed?

MATTHEW 8:8 _____

5. At what two things did Jesus marvel at times?

MATTHEW 8:10; MARK 6:6 _____

The man who showed great faith here was not a Jew, conditioned by experience, prophets and the Old Testament, but a Gentile.

6. Was the woman in Matthew 15 who also showed great faith a Jewess or a Gentile?

MATTHEW 15:22, 28 _____

7. Was Jesus to be a light for the Jews alone, the Gentiles alone, or for all?

ISAIAH 42:6; JOHN 8:12 _____

Abraham had been justified by faith, but hosts of his natural descendants had no faith.

8. What has been the result of Israel's lack of faith?

ROMANS 11:15, 20 _____

9. Did Jesus make people better or well?

MATTHEW 8:3, 13, 15; 9:7, etc. _____

10. How did Jesus work cures in cases of demon possession?

MATTHEW 8:16 _____

11. For Timothy's frequent illnesses, what did Paul recommend: Jesus' method of healing, James' suggestion (JAMES 5:14, 15), the modern "faith healing" method or "wine" (medicine)?

I TIMOTHY 5:23 _____

God-given faith, even for bodily healing, seems nevertheless to be clearly scriptural (I CORINTHIANS 12:9).

12. Would you call Jesus' requirements for discipleship high, medium or low?

MATTHEW 8:19-22 _____

The man in verse 21 evidently wanted to wait until his father's death to follow Jesus.

13. Should we expect smooth sailing simply because Jesus is with us?

MATTHEW 8:23, 24; I PETER 4:12 _____

14. What did Jesus say to His disciples, in contrast to His words to the centurion in verse 10?

MATTHEW 8:26 _____

15. In addition to physical illness, what now is seen to be subject to Jesus?

MATTHEW 8:27 _____

16. Whom did the demons recognize Jesus to be?

MATTHEW 8:29 _____

17. How can we know that these Jews should not have been keeping pigs?

LEVITICUS 11:7, 8 _____

18. Why, probably, did they beseech Jesus to leave the area?

MARK 6:5, 6 _____

Chapter 9 is the Mighty Worker Chapter

19. What great result did faith accomplish in verse 2?

MATTHEW 9:2 _healing   sins forgiven_

20. What more important need did this man have than the cure of his palsy or paralysis?

MATTHEW 9:2 _____

Some people want Jesus to fix up their physical ailments, but they want their sins left alone. Jesus came primarily to save men from sin.

21. Who alone can forgive sins, as the scribes said?

MARK 2:6, 7; ISAIAH 43:25 _God_

22. What is the first evidence of the deity of Jesus in this chapter?

MATTHEW 9:2, 6 _healing by God_

23. What is the second?

MATTHEW 9:4; PSALM 44:21 _that he knows your heart_

24. Why was it not strange for Jesus to be found in the midst of sinners?

MATTHEW 9:10-13; 1:21 _found with those who need help—sinners_

25. How many are in need of Jesus' help?

ROMANS 3:23 _all_

26. Is fasting a ceremony to be regularly observed, or should circumstances mold the action?

MATTHEW 9:15 _circumstances_

Jesus threw ceremonial unreality overboard with these words. Fasting should be the result of real earnestness in a time of need. Otherwise, a fast is a farce.

"The bridegroom," "new cloth," and "new wine" (vv. 14-17) all represent grace; "John," "old garment," and "old bottles (wineskins)" represent the law. Law and grace do not mix.

27. How easy was it to get out of the minds of Jews the idea of putting grace into the old wineskins of the law?

ACTS 15:1, 5; GALATIANS 4:9-11 _difficult_

28. If the power of Christ is to be brought into our lives, with what must it be mixed?

MATTHEW 9:22; HEBREWS 4:2 _faith_

29. How do we know the ruler had that same quality?

MATTHEW 9:18 _he knew his daughter could be brought back to life_

30. What two titles did the blind man apply to Jesus?

MATTHEW 9:27, 28 _Son of David, Lord_

31. What blasphemous explanation did the Pharisees give for Jesus' ability to cast out demons?

MATTHEW 9:34 _Satan_

32. How did Jesus answer this charge at the time?

MATTHEW 9:35 _He went about His business_

33. What phrase indicates Jesus' deep concern for the lost, leaderless people?

MATTHEW 9:36 _Compassion_

34. By whom should laborers be sent into the harvest field?

MATTHEW 9:38 _Lord_

Chapter 10 is the Missions Chapter

35. If we pray for laborers to be sent out, what is apt to happen?

MATTHEW 9:38; 10:1, 5 _We may be sent_

36. Although Jesus chose Judas to be an apostle, what did He know about him?

a. JOHN 6:70, 71 _____

b. JOHN 17:12 _____

37. Is the home circle or the foreign field the place to start giving out the gospel?

MATTHEW 10:5, 6; ACTS 1:8 _____

38. Do the restrictions of this urgent mission apply only here or to every mission?

MATTHEW 10:9, 10; LUKE 22:35, 36 _____

39. What two characteristics should Christian witnesses display among antagonistic unbelievers?

MATTHEW 10:16 _____

40. What hint is given here that their testimony would not long be confined to Israel?

MATTHEW 10:18 _____

41. Are the words of verses 19 and 20 instructions to all preachers and witnesses, or to those facing imprisonment or martyrdom?

MATTHEW 10:19 (first clause) _____

42. How did some people account for the works of Jesus?

MATTHEW 10:25; 9:34 _____

43. How did some account for the wonders of Pentecost?

ACTS 2:13 _____

44. If we confess Christ before men, what will He do?

MATTHEW 10:32 _____

45. And if we deny Him?

MATTHEW 10:33 _____

46. Whom should Christians love even beyond the closest relatives?

MATTHEW 10:37 _____

47. What did Jesus say about the one who does not take up his cross and follow Him?

MATTHEW 10:38 _____

48. What did He say about the one who does even the smallest service for His sake?

MATTHEW 10:42 (last clause) _____

check-up time No. 4

You have now completed your study of chapters 8–10, dealing with the Credentials of the King. Review as before, checking each answer, and if necessary the Scripture text given. Then take the following test to see how well you understand and remember the truths you studied.

In the right-hand margin write "True" or "False" after each of the following statements.

1. Jesus' miracles proved Him to be what He claimed to be.   _____

2. The leper was not quite sure of Jesus' ability to heal him.   _____

3. Jesus marveled at people's love and hatred.   _____

4. Jesus' requirements for discipleship are very high.   _____

5. The most important need of the palsied man was a cure for his palsy.   _____

6. In curing the palsied man, Jesus proved He was God by showing He had the power to forgive sins.   _____

7. The Jews easily gave up the idea of mixing law with grace.   _____

8. The two blind men called Jesus "Lord" and "Son of Abraham."   _____

9. Christian witnesses should be both harmless and wise.   _____

10. Some said Jesus performed miracles by the power of Beelzebub.   _____

Turn to page 96 and check your answers.

The Rejection of the King

MATTHEW 11 AND 12

Chapter 11 is the "No Repentance" Chapter

1. What should have convinced John once for all that Jesus was the Promised One?

MATTHEW 11:2, 3; JOHN 1:33, 34 _____

2. What should the fulfillment of prophecy have taught John?

MATTHEW 11:4, 5; ISAIAH 35:4-6; 61:1, 2a _____

3. Even though John's faith was then wavering, what was Jesus' estimate of him?

MATTHEW 11:9, 11 _____

4. What Old Testament prophet did Jesus quote regarding John?

MALACHI 4:1 _____

5. What two outstanding preachers of the kingdom suffered violence and a violent death?

MATTHEW 11:12; 14:10; 27:35 _____

6. Whom did Jesus consider John to be, in a sense?

MATTHEW 11:14; 17:12, 13 _____

7. In what sense was John the Elijah of Malachi 4:5, 6?

Luke 1:17 _____

8. Did John evidently think of himself as Elijah literally or figuratively?

John 1:21-23 _____

9. To whom did Jesus compare the sulky children who refused to respond either to gaiety or solemnity?

Matthew 11:16 _____

10. What did the Jews do with the message of both John, the "recluse," and Jesus, the "mixer"—accept or reject it?

Matthew 11:18, 19 _____

11. What three Galilean cities will receive worse condemnation in the day of judgment than Tyre, Sidon and Sodom?

Matthew 11:20-24 _____

12. Why will they receive greater condemnation?

Matthew 11:20 _____

13. When a man, even though very intellectual, calls the gospel foolishness, what is true of him?

I Corinthians 1:18 _____

14. Why should no one be upset over the attacks of self-appointed scholars on the Christian faith?

I Corinthians 1:19, 20 _____

15. What basic quality is needed for participation in the kingdom?

Matthew 18:3, 4 _____

16. Since all things are delivered into the hands of Christ, what should every man do?

MATTHEW 11:27; JOHN 3:35, 36 _____

17. How much authority does Jesus possess?

MATTHEW 28:18 _____

"Power" here, is "authority" in A.S.V.

18. Since the Father is revealed only through Jesus, what way must every man take to get to heaven?

MATTHEW 11:27; JOHN 14:6 _____

19. What are the conditions of Jesus' promise of rest to those who labor and are heavy laden?

MATTHEW 11:28 _____

Chapter 12 is the Sabbath Chapter

This chapter might be called the faultfinders' chapter. The Jews repeatedly found fault, either with the Lord or with His disciples.

20. Which commandment did the Pharisees accuse Jesus' disciples of breaking?

MATTHEW 12:1, 2; EXODUS 20:8-11 _____.

Corn, in the Bible, is a general name for grain of any sort.

21. For what people was the Sabbath to serve as a sign?

EZEKIEL 20:12 _____

The Sabbath law in EXODUS 20 was based on the fact that since God worked six days and rested one, man should do likewise.

22. Is the Jewish Sabbath binding on the Christian church since the resurrection of Christ?

ROMANS 14:5, 6; COLOSSIANS 2:16, 17 _____

23. Does it appear that Jesus did or did not use His miraculous powers for the feeding of His own disciples?

MATTHEW 12:1 _____

24. What technical "violation" of the ceremonial law by David did Jesus sanction?

MATTHEW 12:3, 4; I SAMUEL 21:5, 6 _____

25. By the priests in the temple?

MATTHEW 12:5; NUMBERS 28:8-10 _____

26. Was the Sabbath made for man, or man for the Sabbath?

MARK 2:27 _____

27. Who is Lord of the Sabbath day?

MATTHEW 12:8 _____

28. What question regarding the Sabbath did the Pharisees ask Jesus next?

MATTHEW 12:9, 10 _____

29. What technical "violation" of the Sabbath would the most legalistic Jew commit?

MATTHEW 12:11 _____

30. How did Jesus prove His teaching regarding the Sabbath to be correct, and to have God's approval?

MATTHEW 12:13 _____

31. What effect did this have on the Pharisees?

MATTHEW 12:14 _____

32. Did Jesus indicate that at His first coming He would insist and resist, or be meek and mild, regarding His rights?

MATTHEW 12:16, 19, 20 _____

33. If the Jews rejected Him, to whom would He turn?

MATTHEW 12:18, 21 _____

34. What did Jesus' bitterest enemies among His contemporaries admit?

MATTHEW 12:24 _____

"Devils" should be "demons," as in A.S.V.

35. What did they deny?

MATTHEW 12:24, 28 _____

36. Since Satan is really very wise and crafty, how good was the Pharisees' argument that he was casting out his own demons?

MATTHEW 12:25, 26 _____

37. What did Jesus say was proved by His casting out demons by the Spirit of God?

MATTHEW 12:28 _____

38. What two things did Jesus evidently intend to do regarding Satan?

MATTHEW 12:29b _____

39. What did Jesus characterize as "blasphemy against the Holy Ghost"?

MATTHEW 12:31, 32 (compare verse 24) _____

They were attributing to the devil the work evidently that of the Spirit of God.

Jesus was in a veil of flesh, and in spite of His wondrous works they were blind to His glory. But in the case of the Holy Spirit, no such plea could be made. The Spirit works in an unmistakable way. He makes men holy. When it comes to confounding the Holy Spirit with the vile spirit, this is willfully insulting Deity. This is spiritual rottenness and there is no forgiveness. The sin of blasphemy against the Spirit is one that few people could now commit. One who had committed it would have a heart so hard he would never have a desire to come to Christ. If one has such a desire (JOHN 6:37), it is proof he knows nothing of this sin of blasphemy.

40. Whether good or bad, where do the things men say and do, come from?

MATTHEW 12:33-35 _____

41. What was the one great remaining sign of Jesus' authority yet to be given?

MATTHEW 12:38-40 _____

42. What did the men of Nineveh do that the Jews of Jesus' generation refused to do?

MATTHEW 12:41 _____

43. Does Jesus' story of the unclean spirit indicate reformation or regeneration?

MATTHEW 12:43-45 _____

When the Holy Spirit has come in, demons cannot enter the life. Christians may be influenced by demons, but not possessed. This parable pictures a person who has cleaned up morally. The evil spirit has left him, but there is nothing to prevent the spirit returning with more of his kind. This was the moral condition of the Jewish nation. The spirit of idolatry had gone out for a season and they were boasting of their forms and traditions. Because they refused to let Christ in, evil would soon return to them in sevenfold energy.

44. Who are the members of the spiritual family of Christ and of God?

MATTHEW 12:48-50 _____

You have now finished your study of chapters 11 and 12, dealing with the Rejection of the King. Review as before, checking each answer, and if necessary the Scripture passage or passages given. Then take the following test to see how well you understand and remember the truths studied.

In the right-hand margin write "True" or "False" after each of the following statements.

1. John's faith that Jesus was the Messiah wavered. _____

2. Jesus quoted Hosea regarding John. _____

3. The Jews accepted the message of John and rejected that of Jesus. _____

4. Humility is needed for participation in the kingdom. _____

5. Jesus promised rest to those who go to the church for it. _____

6. The Pharisees accused Jesus' disciples of breaking the commandment about God's name. _____

7. Ezekiel says the Sabbath was to serve as a sign for all men. _____

8. David once ate the tabernacle showbread. _____

9. Jesus said even a strict Jew would rescue his sheep from a pit on the Sabbath. _____

10. The Pharisees denied that Jesus cast out demons. _____

Turn to page 96 and check your answers.

The Parables of the King

MATTHEW 13 AND 14

Chapter 13 is the Kingdom Chapter

This chapter contains seven parables of the kingdom of heaven (eight, if the one in verse 52 is included). These parables are here applied to conditions in the present Church Age, although there may be other applications. The kingdom of heaven is here now, in a "mystery" sense. The seven parables are as follows:

(1) The Soils—verses 4-8, 18-23
(2) The Tares and Wheat— verses 24-30, 37-43
(3) The Mustard Seed— verses 31, 32
(4) The Leaven—verse 33
(5) The Hid Treasure—verse 44
(6) The Pearl—verses 45, 46
(7) The Dragnet—verses 47-50

1. To whom were the first four parables addressed?

MATTHEW 13:2 _____

2. The last three?

MATTHEW 13:36 _____

3. In the first parable, what is the "seed"?

MATTHEW 13:4, 19 _____

4. What is the "wayside"?

MATTHEW 13:4, 19 _____

5. What do the "fowls" represent?

Matthew 13:4, 19 _____

The hardened soil of verse 4 represents those fortified against the good seed, those who are blinded by the devil and so do not accept the truth in a saving sense.

6. Who are the shallow-soil hearers of the Word?

Matthew 13:5, 6, 20, 21 _____

This is the emotional hearer, who is impulsive but has no real depth and cannot stand the heat of ridicule.

7. Who are the thorny-ground hearers?

Matthew 13:7, 22 _____

These are the people dominated by the world and, like the soil that is already filled with weeds, their hearts are not available to the good seed.

8. Who are the good or prepared-ground hearers?

Matthew 13:8, 23 _____

9. Of the four kinds of ground, in how many were there root and fruit?

Matthew 13:4-8, 19-23 _____

10. How do you account for the degrees in fruit bearing?

Matthew 13:8; John 15:2, 5 _____

_____

11. To whom is it given "to know the mysteries of the kingdom"?

Matthew 13:10, 11 _____

12. Why is it given to such?

HEBREWS 4:2 _____

13. Who is the sower in the second parable?

MATTHEW 13:24, 37 _____

14. What is the field?

MATTHEW 13:24, 38 _____

15. What is the seed?

MATTHEW 13:24, 38 _____

Note the contrast with the seed in the first parable.

16. What are the tares?

MATTHEW 13:25, 38 _____

17. Who is the enemy sower?

MATTHEW 13:25, 39 _____

Tares are a most troublesome weed; they look much like wheat in the early stages. They cannot be pulled up without also pulling up the wheat. Tares are bitter and nauseating if eaten. No figure could better set forth the malice and cunning of the devil. Note carefully what the tares represent: children of the wicked one (verse 38), adherents of false teachings. They are mixed in with genuine Christians. It is both dangerous and difficult to root them out.

18. Who, eventually, are to deal with the tares?

MATTHEW 13:41 _____

19. How is the small beginning of Christendom pictured?

MATTHEW 13:31, 32 _____

Here abnormal growth is pictured, as Christendom is abnormally large for the number of true Christians involved.

20. What did the birds stand for in the first parable, and perhaps here too?

MATTHEW 13:4, 19, 32 _____

If the birds that come and roost in the tree are the devil's servants, then we have a picture of Christendom that has made an alliance with the world, even to the point of supporting the devil's servants.

21. Would Jesus' Jewish hearers understand "leaven" to represent something good or evil?

MATTHEW 13:33; EXODUS 12:15-20; 13:3 _____

Leaven is a ferment mixed with dough or other material to make it light. It is corruption in action. False doctrine is to permeate the kingdom, or Christendom.

22. How completely did Jesus say the leaven would permeate the meal?

MATTHEW 13:33 _____

23. How prevalent today is false teaching in Christendom, including Roman Catholicism, Eastern Orthodox Catholicism, liberal and orthodox Protestantism, and the cults?

II TIMOTHY 4:3, 4 _____

24. Do other prophecies concerning the end of the age agree or disagree with the interpretation of leaven as corrupting doctrine?

I TIMOTHY 4:1, 2; II TIMOTHY 3:1-7; II PETER 2:1-3 _____

25. With what emotion does the man sell all and buy the field in which the treasure is hid?

MATTHEW 13:44 _____

26. Who went to the cross with this same emotion?

HEBREWS 12:2 _____

27. What price did Christ pay for Israel's redemption?

Isaiah 49:6, 7; I Peter 1:18, 19 _____

Israel is a treasure (Exodus 19:5) "hid in," and now scattered through, the world. In a sense, to redeem Israel Christ has redeemed the world (I Timothy 2:6).

28. What price did Christ pay to redeem the Church?

Matthew 13:46; I Corinthians 7:23; Ephesians 5:25 _____

_____

29. By right of purchase, to whom does the Church belong?

Matthew 13:46 _____

30. The dragnet when full contains what two kinds of fish?

Matthew 13:48 _____

31. What do the two kinds of fish represent?

Matthew 13:49 _____

Note the similarity between the dragnet parable and the tares parable (see 13:38-43). Note also that in the sower parable, the evil is *outside;* in the tares parable, *alongside;* in the mustard seed parable, *topside;* and in the leaven parable, *inside.* The last three parables, however, deal respectively with the redemption of Israel, the redemption of the Church, and the separation of mere professors from genuine believers.

32. In giving Bible instruction, what should every scribe (or teacher) bring out?

Matthew 13:52 _____

Chapter 14 is the Bread Chapter

33. How great an impression did Jesus' miracles make on Herod?

MATTHEW 14:1, 2 _____

34. Why did Herod imprison John?

MATTHEW 14:3, 4 _____

35. What was Herod willing to do to honor his oath and save face with his guests?

MATTHEW 14:9, 10 _____

36. What did Jesus' disciples advise doing with the hungry crowd?

MATTHEW 14:15 _____

37. How did Jesus brush aside their flimsy excuses for inaction?

MATTHEW 14:16 _____

38. What was the disciples' reaction to Jesus' suggestion?

MATTHEW 14:17 _____

39. Where did the power to meet the need really lie?

MATTHEW 14:18 _____

40. If we want to "feed the multitudes," whose blessing must we have?

MATTHEW 14:19 _____

41. Did Jesus go directly to the multitude, or use mere men?

MATTHEW 14:19 _____

42. For what purpose did Jesus go up into the mountain alone?

MATTHEW 14:23 _____

43. When we follow Jesus' directions exactly, will we always have smooth sailing?

MATTHEW 14:22, 24 _____

44. On what simple word of Jesus did Peter step out of the boat in faith?

MATTHEW 14:29 _____

45. When Peter saw the wind instead of the Lord, what happened?

MATTHEW 14:30 _____

46. When Peter began to sink, what wise thing did he do?

MATTHEW 14:30 _____

47. What fault did Jesus find with Peter here?

MATTHEW 14:31 _____

48. Of what profound truth were the disciples convinced after this episode?

MATTHEW 14:33 _____

check-up time No. 6

You have now concluded your study of chapters 13 and 14, dealing with the Parables of the King. Review as previously, checking each answer, and if necessary the Scripture given. Then take the following test to see how well you understand and remember the truths studied.

In the right-hand margin write "True" or "False" after each of the following statements.

1. The last three parables in MATTHEW 13:1-50 were addressed to Jesus' disciples. _____

2. The fowls in the first parable represent the wicked one. _____

3. Knowledge of the mysteries of the kingdom, and the like, is given to those with great learning. _____

4. In the parable of the tares, the field is the world. _____

5. Qualified leaders should carefully root out the tares. _____

6. Sometimes leaven represents good and sometimes evil. _____

7. False teaching is prevalent in Christendom today. _____

8. The price Christ paid for the Church was Himself. _____

9. The dragnet contained big and little fish. _____

10. Jesus went up into the mountain alone to pray. _____

Turn to page 96 and check your answers.

The Purpose of the King

MATTHEW 15–17

Chapter 15 is the Faith and Formality Chapter

1. What did the scribes and Pharisees evidently think was of supreme importance?

MATTHEW 15:1-3 _____

2. What did Jesus think was most important?

MATTHEW 15:3, 6 _____

3. Who were the real transgressors?

MATTHEW 15:2, 3 _____

Jesus gave them a specific example.

4. In the law, what did God require of children?

MATTHEW 15:4; EXODUS 20:12 _____

To "honor" parents included support of them when in need. These religious leaders had found a way to avoid obedience to the law of God.

5. What does Mark say the Jewish leaders permitted children to say to their parents?

MARK 7:11, 12 _____

"Corban" means devoted, or given for some sacred use.

6. What did Jesus call men who talk about having clean hands and then lay foul hands on the Word of God?

MATTHEW 15:7 _____

7. How did Jesus meet their hypocrisy and traditionalism?

MATTHEW 15:7 _____

8. What did Jesus say about the worship of those who have a mere mouth or lip religion?

MATTHEW 15:8, 9 _____

9. What did Jesus mean by "that which goeth into the mouth"?

MATTHEW 15:11, 17 _____

10. What did He mean by "that which cometh out of the mouth"?

MATTHEW 15:11, 18, 19 _____

No amount of washing or food-purifying ceremonies can affect a man's relations with God.

11. How did Jesus characterize those leaders who set God's Word at naught?

MATTHEW 15:14 _____

12. What was Jesus' special mission at this point?

MATTHEW 15:24 _____

13. What quality in this Gentile woman was Jesus evidently intent on bringing out?

MATTHEW 15:28 _____

14. How did Jesus prove His statement, "I have compassion on the multitude" (15:32)?

MATTHEW 15:36, 37 _____

Chapter 16 is the Great Confession Chapter

15. What two sects, usually violently opposed to each other, were yet able to get together against Jesus?

MATTHEW 16:1 _____

16. Why should we study current events?

MATTHEW 16:3 _____

17. What was the sign of the prophet Jonas (Jonah)?

MATTHEW 12:39, 40 _____

18. How did Jesus use the word "leaven" here?

MATTHEW 16:6, 12 _____

19. What did the disciples lack, at least in some degree?

MATTHEW 16:8 _____

20. How important is it to know the true identity of Jesus?

MATTHEW 16:13; JOHN 20:31; I JOHN 5:10-12 _____

21. Why is it illogical to call Jesus a good man while denying His deity?

JOHN 7:12 _____

22. Was there much confusion of error as to Jesus' true identity?

MATTHEW 16:14 _____

23. What was Peter's confession?

MATTHEW 16:16 _____

_____

24. What is one of the basic truths of the gospel?

ACTS 9:20 _____

25. Who teach men this truth?

MATTHEW 16:17; I CORINTHIANS 12:3 _____

26. Was the Church to be built on Peter or on the One whom he had just confessed?

MATTHEW 16:18; I CORINTHIANS 3:11; EPHESIANS 2:19, 20 _____

27. On whom does Peter say the Church is built, himself or Christ?

I PETER 2:4-7 _____

28. To whom, however, were the keys of the kingdom to be given?

MATTHEW 16:19 _____

29. If the kingdom of heaven is the sphere of Christian profession, for what two all-inclusive divisions of humanity did Peter use these keys?

ACTS 2:36-41; 10:43-48 _____

30. Did Peter's power to "bind" or "loose" on earth apply to "whomsoever" or to "whatsoever"?

MATTHEW 16:19 _____

This probably refers to Peter's preaching on Pentecost and in the house of Cornelius.

31. What two vital things did Jesus now say must occur before the Church could be built, or Peter could use the keys?

MATTHEW 16:21 _____

32. Did Jesus know in advance what would happen to Him in Jerusalem, or did it come upon Him unexpectedly?

MATTHEW 16:21 _____

33. For what purpose did Christ come into the world?

MATTHEW 20:28; JOHN 3:14, 15 _____

34. What triumph was to follow His death?

MATTHEW 16:21 _____

35. What was Peter's reaction to Jesus' prediction regarding His death?

MATTHEW 16:22 _____

36. Who, before Peter, had suggested to Jesus this idea of avoiding the cross?

MATTHEW 4:8, 9 _____

It was Satan who said, "Spare thyself," omit the cross, rule the world without it.

37. What words, similar to those spoken earlier to Satan (MATTHEW 4:10), were now addressed to Peter?

MATTHEW 16:23 _____

38. When Peter spoke the words of God, what did Jesus say to him?

MATTHEW 16:17 _____

Here we have a man, who shortly before knew something that only the Father could reveal, now speaking the words of Satan.

39. To really be a disciple, a follower, of Christ, whom must a man deny (say no to)?

MATTHEW 16:24 _____

40. For whose sake should we sacrifice, or yield up, our lives?

MATTHEW 16:25 _____

41. Reward from the Son of Man at His return will be according to what principle?

MATTHEW 16:27 _____

Chapter 17 is the Transfiguration Chapter

42. What promise did Jesus make shortly before His transfiguration?

MATTHEW 16:28—17:2 _____

43. What did Jesus discuss with Moses and Elijah?

LUKE 9:30, 31 _____

44. What was God's testimony concerning Jesus?

MATTHEW 17:5 _____

45. Whom did the three disciples see at the end of this event?

MATTHEW 17:8 _____

46. Why were the disciples unable to cast the demon out of the lunatic boy?

MATTHEW 17:20 _____

47. What two vital predictions did Jesus make again here?

MATTHEW 17:22, 23 _____

check-up time No. 7

You have finished your study of chapters 15–17, dealing with the Purpose of the King. Review as before, checking each answer, and if necessary the Scripture text given. Then take the following test to see how well you understand and remember the truths studied.

In the right-hand margin write "True" or "False" after each of the following statements.

1. The scribes and Pharisees thought the commandment of God to be of supreme importance. _____

2. Jesus called the scribes and Pharisees hypocrites. _____

3. Jesus' original mission was to both Jews and Gentiles. _____

4. Jesus proved His compassion on the hungry multitude by sending His disciples to buy food for them. _____

5. The two opposing sects that made common cause
against Jesus in MATTHEW 16:1 were Pharisees and
Sadducees. _____

6. Jesus used "leaven" in MATTHEW 16 to represent
the doctrine of demons. _____

7. There were many varying opinions regarding the
true identity of Jesus. _____

8. Peter claimed the Church was built on himself. _____

9. The keys of the Church were to be given to Peter. _____

10. Jesus discussed His decease with Moses and Elijah. _____

Turn to page 96 and check your answers.

The Standards of the King

MATTHEW 18–20

Chapter 18 is the Humility Chapter

1. What did Jesus use as an object lesson in humility?

MATTHEW 18:1-3 _____

2. What quality did Jesus here indicate is indispensable for entrance into the kingdom of heaven?

MATTHEW 18:3, 4 _____

3. What was Jesus' answer to the disciples' question in verse 1?

MATTHEW 18:4 _____

4. What did Jesus say of the person who makes a holy and useful life more difficult for others to live?

MATTHEW 18:6 _____

The word "offend" means "cause to stumble."

5. How far should we go in our carefulness not to cause another to stumble?

I CORINTHIANS 8:13 _____

6. What does Paul say we ought to do with the flesh and its desires?

GALATIANS 5:24 _____

7. What sort of people did the Son of Man come to save?

MATTHEW 18:11 _____

8. Over whom did the Lord rejoice particularly?

MATTHEW 18:12-14 _____

9. What does Isaiah say is true of all of us?

ISAIAH 53:6 _____

10. What is sometimes the cause of people going astray?

JEREMIAH 50:6 _____

11. Under the circumstances indicated, if your brother listens to you, what have you gained?

MATTHEW 18:15 _____

If your motive is to cram his words down his throat, leave the matter alone. If it is to restore broken fellowship, you may gain your brother.

12. If he will not listen to you, what should you do?

MATTHEW 18:16 _____

13. If he will not listen to others what then?

MATTHEW 18:17 _____

14. How many persons gathered in Christ's name are needed to insure His presence in their midst, to guide them in praying?

MATTHEW 18:19, 20 _____

15. What is the great secret of all-prevailing prayer?

JUDE 20; EPHESIANS 6:18 _____

16. How many times did Jesus say we should forgive a brother?

MATTHEW 18:21, 22 _____

This suggests no limit in forgiving others.

17. Did the first servant owe his master, the king, a large or small sum?

MATTHEW 18:24, 32 _____

18. Did the second servant owe the first servant a large or small sum?

MATTHEW 18:28 _____

19. In the first instance, was the king righteous or gracious?

MATTHEW 18:25 _____

20. Later, was he righteous or gracious?

MATTHEW 18:27 _____

In righteousness, God could demand of us full payment for every sin; but instead, in grace, He offers us full forgiveness through Christ.

21. Would you say the king's forgiveness of the first servant was potential or actual?

MATTHEW 18:32-34 _____

22. How can we be sure this servant was a fraud—not a true servant at all—and does not represent a genuine believing Christian?

MATTHEW 18:32-35 _____

Chapter 19 is the Marriage Chapter

23. With what motive did the Pharisees approach Jesus here?

MATTHEW 19:3 _____

24. Who gave approval to the Genesis account of creation?

MATTHEW 19:4 _____

25. What had God said about the marriage relationship at the very beginning?

GENESIS 2:23, 24 _____

_____

26. Is marriage a mere agreement between a man and a woman, or a union which God has effected?

MATTHEW 19:6 _____

27. What is the only scriptural ground upon which a Christian can get a divorce?

MATTHEW 19:9 _____

28. Since Jesus made wedlock so much like a "padlock," to what extreme did the disciples go?

MATTHEW 19:10 _____

29. What class alone did Jesus say could "receive this saying"?

MATTHEW 19:11 _____

30. How many classes of eunuchs did Jesus indicate there were?

MATTHEW 19:12 _____

31. What two contrasting words did Jesus use concerning little children and adults, in getting them into the kingdom?

MATTHEW 19:14; LUKE 14:23 _____

32. What mistaken idea did this man have about getting eternal life?

MATTHEW 19:16 _____

33. Did Jesus mean to imply that He was not good, or that He was not God?

MATTHEW 19:17; JOHN 8:29, 46; MATTHEW 9:6 _____

Jesus wanted the man to see that if He was "good," He must then be God.

34. What did Jesus tell this man to do?

MATTHEW 19:17 _____

35. Should the mere recital of the manward commandments of God have convicted this man and shown him the impossibility of his keeping the law?

MATTHEW 19:18, 19 _____

36. What absurd claim did he make, nevertheless?

MATTHEW 19:20 _____

37. In a further effort to convict the man, what did Jesus tell him to do, ultimately?

MATTHEW 19:21 (last four words) _____

38. Even after all this, what did the man do?

MATTHEW 19:22 _____

The law is a mirror, useful to show us ourselves as we really are (ROMANS 7:12, 13; 3:20).

39. If believers forsake all for the sake of Christ, what recompense will they have?

MATTHEW 19:29 _____

Chapter 20 is the Laborers' Chapter

Jesus wanted to teach His disciples not to be anxious about compensation for Christian service. The time to get their reward was at the end of the day, and they should leave it all to their Master's grace.

40. Did the laborers seek the employer, or the reverse?

MATTHEW 20:1 _____

41. Did the first laborers receive what was agreed upon, or more or less?

MATTHEW 20:2, 10 _____

42. Did the laborers here represent unsaved men working for salvation, or saved men working for the Lord?

EPHESIANS 2:8-10 _____

43. Is it better for believers to serve the Lord for a stipulated compensation, or leave it to Him?

MATTHEW 20:12, 15 _____

44. How many times before this in Matthew had Jesus foretold His death and resurrection?

MATTHEW 20:17-19 _____

45. How ambitious were Zebedee's wife and children?

MATTHEW 20:20, 21 _____

46. To what extent did Jesus say James and John would share with Him?

MATTHEW 20:23 _____

47. What did Jesus say is the way to greatness among Christians?

MATTHEW 20:26 _____

"Minister" means "servant."

48. What did Jesus say here was His purpose in coming into this world?

MATTHEW 20:28 _____

49. What was Jesus planning to give as "a ransom for many"?

MATTHEW 20:28 _____

check-up time No. 8

You have finished your study of chapters 18–20, dealing with the Standards of the King. Review as previously, checking each answer and if necessary the Scripture references. Then take the following test to see how well you understand and remember the truths considered.

In the right-hand margin write "True" or "False" after each of the following statements.

1. To enter the kingdom, one must have humility. _____

2. Paul says we ought to starve the flesh. _____

3. People are sometimes led astray by their leaders or guides. _____

4. Jesus said we should forgive a brother seventy times seven times. _____

5. The king's forgiveness of the first servant in MATTHEW 18 was potential. _____

6. In MATTHEW 19, the Pharisees approached Jesus to flatter Him. _____

7. Jesus spoke of four classes of eunuchs. _____

8. The man who addressed Jesus as "Good Master" asked what good thing he should do for eternal life. _____

9. In MATTHEW 20, the laborers sought the employer. _____

10. James and John were exceedingly ambitious. _____

Turn to page 96 and check your answers.

The Acclaim
of the King

MATTHEW 21–23

Chapter 21 is the Triumphal Entry Chapter

1. For what purpose had Jesus just said He had come into the world?

MATTHEW 20:28 _____

2. Had He any thought of being received at Jerusalem as an earthly king?

MATTHEW 20:18 _____

3. When the prophet foretold this entry into Jerusalem, what did he say the King would be?

ZECHARIAH 9:9 _____

4. Did this prophet indicate the King would at this time come humbly or gloriously?

ZECHARIAH 9:9 _____

5. When the King comes to overthrow all opposition and to reign, what will He be riding?

REVELATION 19:11-16 _____

6. What did many in the multitude mistakenly think Jesus was coming to Jerusalem to do?

MARK 11:10 _____

7. What were Jesus' emotions at this point?

LUKE 19:41, 42 _____

8. What was the multitude's opinion of Jesus?

MATTHEW 21:11 _____

9. What two contrasting designations of the temple are given here?

MATTHEW 21:13 _____

10. What was the attitude of the chief priests and scribes at this point?

MATTHEW 21:15 _____

11. What did Jesus find on the fig tree: fruit, leaves, or both or neither?

MATTHEW 21:19 _____

The fig tree is symbolic of Israel, the leaves of religious pretense.

12. Why were the chief priests and elders unwilling to answer Jesus' question about John's baptism?

MATTHEW 21:25-27 _____

_____

13. In the parable of the two sons, whom does the repentant first son represent?

MATTHEW 21:31 _____

14. The polite second son?

MATTHEW 21:23, 31 _____

15. Had the householder gone to great lengths on his vineyard?

MATTHEW 21:33 _____

16. How does Isaiah describe the fruit of Israel, the Lord's vineyard?

Isaiah 5:1-7 (verses 2, 4) _____

17. What did the husbandmen plan to do to the householder's son?

Matthew 21:38 _____

18. Whom did Jesus mean by the "husbandmen"?

Matthew 21:41, 45 _____

19. What did Jesus say would be taken from Israel and given to others?

Matthew 21:43 _____

Chapter 22 is the Marriage Feast Chapter

This parable indicates the kingdom of heaven has to do with a period during which messengers are to go into the highways and byways and bid all to a feast of divine grace.

20. What was the response of those first invited?

Matthew 22:3 _____

21. What was their reaction when the invitation was repeated?

Matthew 22:5 _____

22. What was done to the king's servants?

Matthew 22:6 _____

23. What did the king do to these murderers and their city (Jerusalem)?

Matthew 22:7 _____

24. How was the wedding furnished with guests?

MATTHEW 22:10 _____

25. What great messenger to those in the highways and byways was formerly a great persecutor of Christians?

EPHESIANS 3:1, 7, 8 _____

26. What did the "gate-crasher" lack?

MATTHEW 22:12 _____

The wedding garment, customarily provided by the king, represents the robe of righteousness (ISAIAH 61:10) God offers the sinner in Christ (II CORINTHIANS 5:21; REVELATION 7:9).

27. How do we know the Pharisees and Herodians were insincere here?

MATTHEW 22:15-17 _____

28. How did Jesus silence them?

MATTHEW 22:21 _____

29. What doctrine of Jesus were the Sadducees trying to ridicule with their question?

MATTHEW 22:23, 28 _____

30. Of what two things did Jesus say these "liberals" were ignorant?

MATTHEW 22:29 _____

31. How did Jesus silence these Sadducees?

MATTHEW 22:30 _____

32. From what Old Testament book did Jesus quote to the lawyer the first and great commandment?

MATTHEW 22:35-38; DEUTERONOMY 6:5 _____

33. And the second, "like unto it"?

MATTHEW 22:39; LEVITICUS 19:18 _____

34. How important did Jesus say these two commandments were?

MATTHEW 22:40 _____

35. What question did Jesus ask the Pharisees?

MATTHEW 22:42 _____

36. Whom did Jesus quote to show their answer was inadequate?

PSALM 110:1 _____

A man does not normally refer to his son as "my Lord."

37. What is the real truth about the identity of David's son?

MATTHEW 16:16; JOHN 20:31 _____

Chapter 23 is the Hypocrite Chapter

38. Who did Jesus say were Moses' "successors"?

MATTHEW 23:1, 2 _____

39. What did Jesus tell the people to do in this connection?

MATTHEW 23:3 _____

40. What did He warn them not to do?

MATTHEW 23:3 _____

41. What noticeable lack was there along with their great show of authority?

MATTHEW 23:4 _____

42. What three titles did Jesus warn against here?

MATTHEW 23:8, 9, 10 _____

43. What title do all believers share alike?

MATTHEW 23:8 _____

This is not to be understood as forbidding any believer to be a teacher of other believers (I CORINTHIANS 12:28; EPHESIANS 4:11), but as a warning against pride and arrogance.

44. What quality in a leader is extremely becoming?

MATTHEW 23:12 _____

45. What did Jesus repeatedly call the scribes and Pharisees in this chapter?

MATTHEW 23:13, 14, 15, 23, etc. _____

46. What was His first charge against them?

MATTHEW 23:13 _____

_____

47. Did Jesus approve or disapprove of their proselytizing program?

MATTHEW 23:15 _____

48. Did He approve or condemn their intricate scale of oaths?

MATTHEW 23:16-22 _____

49. Of what hypocrisy regarding martyred prophets did Jesus accuse them?

MATTHEW 23:29, 30 _____

_____

50. What did He prophesy they themselves would do?

MATTHEW 23:34 _____

51. Of what great sin did Jesus say Jerusalem was guilty?

MATTHEW 23:37 _____

52. What was His attitude toward Jerusalem, nevertheless?

MATTHEW 23:37 _____

You have completed your study of chapters 21–23, dealing with the Acclaim of the King. Review as before, checking each answer, and if necessary the Scripture references. Then take the following test to see how well you understand and remember the truths covered.

In the right-hand margin write "True" or "False" after each of the following statements.

1. It was Isaiah who foretold that the King, when He entered Jerusalem on an ass, would have salvation. _____

2. At the "triumphal entry," the multitude believed Jesus was the Son of God. _____

3. The chief priests and elders told Jesus they knew John's baptism was from heaven. _____

4. The repentant first son in MATTHEW 21 represented the publicans and harlots. _____

5. Those first invited to the marriage feast refused to go. _____

6. The city Jesus said the king burned up was Babylon. _____

7. The "gate-crasher" at the marriage feast lacked a wedding garment. _____

8. It was the Sadducees who asked Jesus the question about the tribute money. _____

9. Jesus said the scribes and Pharisees were Moses' "successors." _____

10. Repeatedly, Jesus called the scribes and Pharisees "hypocrites." _____

Turn to page 96 and check your answers.

The Return of the King

MATTHEW 24 AND 25

Chapter 24 is the Second Coming Chapter

1. Just before leaving the temple, what had Jesus said?

MATTHEW 23:38 _____

2. What three questions did the disciples ask Jesus here?

MATTHEW 24:3

a. _____

b. _____

c. _____

Seven classes of signs of the age are given in this discourse.

I. The Infernal Signs (24:5, 23-26)

3. What will some cults try to do in the last days?

MATTHEW 24:5 _____

4. What should be our reaction to anyone who says Christ has returned, but is in some particular locality?

MATTHEW 24:23-26 _____

II. The National Signs (24:6-10)

5. What national or political signs point to the culmination of the age?

MATTHEW 24:6, 7 _____

6. How do the wars, pestilences, and the like at first, compare with the end time?

MATTHEW 24:8 _____

7. What will be the effect of these awful conditions on human society?

MATTHEW 24:10 _____

8. What kind of treatment may God's true ambassadors expect under these conditions?

MATTHEW 24:9 _____

III. The Religious Signs (24:11-13)

9. What are the religious signs of the approaching end of the age?

MATTHEW 24:11, 12 _____

_____

10. May we expect universal righteousness or even fervent religion in the church prior to the Lord's return?

MATTHEW 24:12; II TIMOTHY 3:1-5 _____

11. How much of a following may we expect the false teachers to get?

MATTHEW 24:11 _____

IV. The Missionary Sign (24:14)

12. What will be the missionary sign?

MATTHEW 24:14 _____

Only God can say when the "witness" has been sufficiently borne.

13. What Old Testament prophet speaks of the "abomination of desolation" (probably the image of the man of sin of II THESSALONIANS 2:3, 4)?

MATTHEW 24:15 _____

14. Does the Great Tribulation, as described here, seem to have special reference to Israel, the world, the Gentiles or the Church?

MATTHEW 24:15, 16, 20 _____

Note references to "the holy place," "Judea," and "the sabbath day."

15. How will this Great Tribulation compare with other times of trouble?

MATTHEW 24:21 _____

16. May Christ's coming be considered the gradual diffusion of Christian principles, or is it a sudden event?

MATTHEW 24:27 _____

17. Will it be public or private?

MATTHEW 24:27, 30; REVELATION 1:7 _____

18. What will be done about the Lord's elect when Christ returns?

MATTHEW 24:31 _____

V. The Jewish Sign (24:32-34)

19. When Israel begins to bud again as a nation, after all the years of dispersion, of what is it a sign? ("It" in verse 33 is "he" in A.S.V.)

MATTHEW 24:32, 33 _____

The preservation of the Jews throughout these many centuries without a national home is the miracle of history.

VI. The Social Signs (24:37-44)

20. What will be the social signs at the end of the age?

MATTHEW 24:37-39 _____

21. What success did Noah have in converting the world outside his own family?

MATTHEW 24:38; II PETER 2:5 _____

22. In what state will the world be before Jesus returns?

MATTHEW 24:37 _____

23. What will happen to society when Jesus comes?

MATTHEW 24:40, 41 _____

This is not the rapture. Those "taken" here are taken away for judgment.

24. What is the practical lesson here?

MATTHEW 24:42-44 _____

VII. The Ecclesiastical Sign (24:45-51)

25. What will be the ecclesiastical sign?

MATTHEW 24:48; II PETER 3:3, 4 _____

26. What does God expect of His servants?

MATTHEW 24:45 _____

27. What will every minister want to be found doing when Jesus comes?

MATTHEW 24:46, 47 _____

28. What kind of servant did Jesus call the man who pushes away the teaching concerning His second advent?

MATTHEW 24:48 _____

29. To what kind of conduct is this attitude apt to lead?

MATTHEW 24:49 _____

30. In what class will such a servant find himself when Jesus comes?

MATTHEW 24:51 _____

31. Will the day of Jesus' coming be a joyful day for all leaders in the Christian church?

MATTHEW 24:51 _____

Chapter 25 is the Virgins' Chapter

32. Of what is the lamp a type in Scripture?

MATTHEW 25:1; PSALM 119:105 _____

33. Of what is oil a type?

MATTHEW 25:3, 4; PSALM 45:7 _____

Christ was anointed with the Holy Spirit (JOHN 1:33), and preached the gospel, or glad tidings (LUKE 4:18).

34. Who enables men to understand spiritual truth?

I CORINTHIANS 2:10, 13, 14 _____

35. Into what two classes had Jesus divided men at the beginning of His ministry?

MATTHEW 7:24, 26 _____

36. What was the fatal deficiency of the foolish virgins?

MATTHEW 25:3 _____

37. What did Jesus definitely say to the foolish virgins?

MATTHEW 25:12 _____

38. What wise provision did the wise virgins, or true believers, make?

MATTHEW 25:4; JOHN 7:39 _____

39. What were both the wise and foolish represented as doing?

MATTHEW 25:5 _____

40. How long a time may it be necessary to wait?

MATTHEW 25:19 _____

41. What is prophesied regarding the attitude of many in the last days toward the second coming of Christ?

MATTHEW 24:48; II PETER 3:3, 4, 9 _____

42. What alerting cry was made at midnight?

MATTHEW 25:6 _____

43. To whom did the foolish go for oil?

MATTHEW 25:8 _____

44. Who gives the Holy Spirit, Christian believers or Christ (the Bride or the Bridegroom)?

MATTHEW 25:8, 9; JOHN 1:33; 7:37-39 _____

45. What is the best Christian believers can do? (Two things)

PHILIPPIANS 2:15, 16 _____

_____

46. When the saved were in, what did the Lord do?

MATTHEW 25:10 _____

47. Was any second chance offered the foolish?

MATTHEW 25:11, 12 _____

48. Who is the man who has gone into the far country?

MATTHEW 25:14; MARK 16:19 _____

49. What sort of goods did He entrust to His servants?

MATTHEW 25:14; ROMANS 12:6-8 _____

Not all have the same ability, but all serve the same Lord and all are responsible to use for His glory the powers He has given them.

50. Which of the three servants put their talents to use?

MATTHEW 25:16, 17 _____

51. What is every Christian expected to do with his gift?

I PETER 4:10 _____

52. On what principle did the master reward the first two servants —their ability, their gifts, or their faithfulness?

MATTHEW 25:21, 23 _____

53. What did the one-talent man do with his gift—something or nothing?

MATTHEW 25:24, 25 _____

54. How responsible does Jesus hold the one-talent man?

MATTHEW 25:27 _____

55. When Jesus comes in His glory, who will accompany Him?

MATTHEW 25:31; I THESSALONIANS 3:13 _____

56. Who are to be gathered before Him then?

MATTHEW 25:32; JOEL 3:12 _____

"Heathen" is the same as "nations."

57. What three classes are referred to in this judgment of living nations?

MATTHEW 25:33, 40 _____

58. What kingdom is this?

MATTHEW 25:34; LUKE 1:32, 33 _____

59. On what basis are both sheep and goats judged—their treatment of whom?

MATTHEW 25:35, 36, 42, 43 _____

60. How have they shown their attitude toward Christ?

MATTHEW 25:40, 45 _____

61. Who are Christ's brethren according to the flesh?

ROMANS 9:3-5 _____

62. For whom was the "everlasting fire" prepared?

MATTHEW 25:41 _____

Some deliberately cast in their lot with the devil and his followers.

63. What is the duration both of the "punishment" of the lost or unrighteous, and of the "life" of the saved or righteous?

MATTHEW 25:46 _____

The same Greek word in verse 46 is translated "everlasting" and "eternal."

check-up time No. 10

You have now finished your study of chapters 24 and 25, dealing with the Return of the King. Review as formerly, checking each answer, and if necessary the Bible passage given. Then take the following test to see how well you understand and recall the truths studied.

In the right-hand margin write "True" or "False" after each of the following statements.

1. One question the disciples asked Jesus was, "Is it lawful to give tribute unto Caesar, or not?" _____

2. One of the national signs of Christ's return concerns pestilences. _____

3. The missionary sign concerns the preaching of the gospel of the kingdom. _____

4. Just after Christ returns, the elect will be scattered throughout the world. _____

5. In MATTHEW 24, the vine is used as a symbol of Israel. _____

6. Jesus said the servant who avoids the doctrine of the second coming is evil. _____

7. The lamp is used as a type of the Word of God. _____

8. The foolish virgins lacked the Word of God. _____

9. Only the first servant put his talents to use. _____

10. The everlasting fire was prepared for the devil and his angels. _____

Turn to page 96 and check your answers.

The Condemnation of the King

Matthew 26

Chapter 26 is the Betrayal Chapter

1. What three groups plotted against Jesus?

Matthew 26:3 _____

2. In spite of their wicked devices, what was being carried out?

Proverbs 19:21; Acts 2:23 _____

3. What was the disciples' opinion regarding the expensive ointment poured on Jesus' head?

Matthew 26:8 _____

4. What was Jesus' opinion?

Matthew 26:10 _____

5. What did Jesus mean by "Me ye have not always"?

Matthew 26:11; John 16:28 _____

6. What did Jesus indicate was in the woman's mind when she anointed Him?

Matthew 26:12 _____

7. How famous did Jesus say this act would become?

Matthew 26:13 _____

8. What "gospel" did Jesus refer to here?

MATTHEW 26:13; MARK 1:1; I CORINTHIANS 15:1-4 _____

9. To whom did Judas make his offer to betray Jesus?

MATTHEW 26:14, 15 _____

10. How was Judas received by these leaders?

MARK 14:11 _____

11. In one sense, whose "hour" was this?

LUKE 22:53 _____

12. In another sense, whose "time" was it?

MATTHEW 26:18 _____

13. What feast was Jesus eager to keep with His disciples?

MATTHEW 26:18 _____

The Passover pointed forward to Calvary (I CORINTHIANS 5:7).

14. How was Judas foreseen in the Old Testament?

PSALM 41:9 _____

15. What did Jesus say about the man who was going to betray Him?

MATTHEW 26:24 _____

16. How did Judas' salutation differ from that of the others?

MATTHEW 26:22, 25 _____

17. What does this indicate?

I CORINTHIANS 12:3 _____

18. With what words did Jesus let Judas know that He knew him to be the traitor?

MATTHEW 26:25 _____

81

19. Did Judas fall from salvation or from an official position?

ACTS 1:24, 25 _____

20. What did Jesus call Judas?

JOHN 6:70, 71 _____

21. What did John call him?

JOHN 12:6 _____

22. What else did Jesus call him?

JOHN 17:12 _____

23. What did Jesus say the bread represents?

MATTHEW 26:26 _____

24. What does the cup—that is, its contents—represent?

MATTHEW 26:27, 28 _____

25. What is the new testament (more correctly, covenant) based upon?

MATTHEW 26:28 _____

26. What does the Lord's Supper say to us as to the purpose of our Lord's death?

MATTHEW 26:28 _____

27. What was Peter's first step in backsliding?

MATTHEW 26:33 _____

Self-confidence is always the first step away.

28. What did Peter, in effect, say to Jesus?

MATTHEW 26:34, 35 _____

29. What very different scene had these three disciples witnessed a short time earlier?

MATTHEW 26:36-38; 17:1, 2 _____

30. What did they do on the mount, and again here?

LUKE 9:32; MATTHEW 26:40 _____

31. How deeply did this Gethsemane experience affect Jesus?

LUKE 22:44 _____

_____

32. Did Jesus insist on His own will, or was He willing to accept His Father's will?

MATTHEW 26:39 _____

33. What was the "cup" Jesus prayed might pass from Him?

MATTHEW 26:39, 27, 28 _____

His holy soul shrank from being made sin (II CORINTHIANS 5:21), but if there was no other way, He would submit even to that.

34. What two things did Jesus say we should do to avoid temptation?

MATTHEW 26:41 _____

35. How many times did He pray this prayer about the cup passing from Him?

MATTHEW 26:44 _____

36. What was the supreme hour toward which He had been headed from the first?

MATTHEW 26:45; JOHN 3:14, 15 _____

37. What was the climax of Judas' treachery?

MATTHEW 26:48, 49 _____

38. Even at the moment of betrayal, how did Jesus address Judas?

MATTHEW 26:50 _____

39. How did Peter (JOHN 18:10) now show himself to be out of touch with Jesus?

MATTHEW 26:51 _____

40. Did Jesus really want deliverance from the cross?

MATTHEW 26:53 _____

41. What was His last miracle before going to the cross?

LUKE 22:51 _____

42. What was Peter's next step in backsliding?

MATTHEW 26:58 _____

43. What may account for his lagging behind?

MATTHEW 26:52 _____

44. In whose company did Peter end up?

MATTHEW 26:58 _____

45. What vital question did the high priest ask Jesus?

MATTHEW 26:63 _____

46. What direct reply did Jesus give?

MATTHEW 26:64a _____

47. What additional statement did Jesus make?

MATTHEW 26:64b _____

48. What altogether mistaken conclusion did the high priest draw?

MATTHEW 26:65 _____

49. What charge did the chief priests and elders and the council make against Jesus?

MATTHEW 26:59, 65, 66 _____

50. Of what penalty did they say He was worthy?

MATTHEW 26:66 _____

51. How did they display their hatred of Him?

MATTHEW 26:67 _____

52. How do you explain their question, "Who is he that smote thee?"

MATTHEW 26:68; LUKE 22:64 _____

53. What was the final result of Peter's association with the Lord's enemies?

MATTHEW 26:69-72 _____

54. Then what happened?

MATTHEW 26:74, 75 _____

55. What melted Peter's heart?

MATTHEW 26:75; LUKE 22:61 _____

56. What did Peter have as a believer, even though wayward, that Judas lacked?

LUKE 22:31, 32 _____

57. What did Peter say later, in vivid contrast to his three denials?

JOHN 21:15-17 _____

58. What was the charge made against Jesus at His Jewish "trial"—that of seeking a throne, or that of claiming equality with God?

MATTHEW 26:63-65; JOHN 5:18 _____

check-up time No. 11

You have completed your study of chapter 26 on the Condemnation of the King. Review as before, checking each answer and if necessary the references furnished. Then take the following test to see how well you understood and now remember the truths studied.

In the right-hand margin write "True" or "False" after each of the following statements.

1. The three groups plotting against Jesus in MATTHEW 26 were chief priests, scribes and Pharisees. _____

2. Jesus said the woman anointed Him for the throne of the kingdom. _____

3. Jesus was eager to keep the Passover with His disciples. _____

4. John called Judas "the son of perdition." _____

5. The new covenant is based on Jesus' shed blood. _____

6. Peter's first step in backsliding was self-confidence. _____

7. Jesus said that to avoid temptation we should flee and pray. _____

8. The vital question the high priest asked Jesus was, "Art thou a king, then?" _____

9. The chief priests and elders and the council charged Jesus with blasphemy. _____

10. A look from Jesus melted Peter's heart. _____

Turn to page 96 and check your answers.

The Triumph of the King

MATTHEW 27 AND 28

Chapter 27 is the Crucifixion Chapter

There were six stages in the trial of Jesus: three Jewish—before Annas, Caiaphas, and the council (Sanhedrin); three Gentile or Roman—before Pilate, Herod, and back to Pilate.

1. What was the charge against Jesus at the Jewish trial?

MATTHEW 26:65, 66 _____

2. When the Jewish leaders found Jesus "guilty [worthy] of death," what did they do next?

MATTHEW 27:1, 2 _____

3. When Judas saw that Jesus was condemned, what change came over him?

MATTHEW 27:3 _____

4. What were the last recorded words of Judas regarding Jesus?

MATTHEW 27:4 _____

5. Who else spoke similarly of Jesus?

MATTHEW 27:24 _____

6. How did Pilate's wife refer to Jesus?

MATTHEW 27:19 _____

7. What evidently was Herod's opinion concerning Him?

Luke 23:14, 15 _____

"Done unto him" is "done by him" in A.S.V. (verse 15).

8. What was the charge against Jesus at the Roman trial?
John 19:12 _____

9. What did one malefactor on the cross say of Him?

Luke 23:41 _____

10. What did the centurion say of Him?

Luke 23:47 _____

Note how bloodthirsty these religious leaders were (Matthew 26:66), and how callous (27:4), and yet how meticulous in some matters (27:6).

11. What reaction did Jesus again give when falsely accused?

Matthew 27:12-14; 26:60-63a _____

12. What kind of person was Barabbas?

Mark 15:7; Luke 23:25 _____

13. Of whom is Barabbas a representative?

John 3:18, 36; I John 5:12 _____

14. What is the great question all of us must answer?

Matthew 27:22a _____

15. What awful guilt did the people assume?

Matthew 27:25 _____

16. Of what are the thorns suggestive?

Matthew 27:29; Genesis 3:17, 18 _____

17. What was Jesus' determination as these indignities were heaped upon Him?

MATTHEW 27:28-30; ISAIAH 50:6, 7 _____

18. What mixture was offered Jesus to dull the pain?

MATTHEW 27:34 _____

Presumably He refused this that He might, with unblunted faculties, deal fully with our sins.

19. With what emotion—sympathy, apathy or antipathy—did each of the three groups mentioned watch Jesus on the cross?

a. MATTHEW 27:36 _____

b. MATTHEW 27:39, 40 _____

c. MATTHEW 27:55, 56 _____

20. What did some suggest that Jesus should do?

MATTHEW 27:40 _____

21. To what doctrine do some still object?

PHILIPPIANS 3:18 _____

22. Why could He not save Himself?

JOHN 3:14-16 _____

23. What change later took place in one of the thieves?

MATTHEW 27:44; LUKE 23:39-42 _____

24. What difference may be noted between the death of Jesus and that of a Christian martyr like Stephen?

MATTHEW 27:46; ACTS 7:54-56 _____

_____

25. Why was Jesus forsaken by God for a time?

MATTHEW 27:46; HABAKKUK 1:13; II CORINTHIANS 5:21 _____

_____

26. Was Jesus' life taken from Him, or did He voluntarily give it up?

MATTHEW 27:50; JOHN 10:18 _____

27. In the rending of the veil of the temple, what fact strongly suggests it was done by God's hand?

MATTHEW 27:51 _____

28. What further proof was soon to be given that God accepted the finished work of Jesus?

ROMANS 4:24, 25 _____

29. What would be still another proof?

JOHN 16:7; ACTS 2:33 _____

30. What did rude soldiers now confess, that religious leaders strongly denied?

MATTHEW 27:54 _____

31. Had Joseph been an out-and-out or a secret disciple?

MATTHEW 27:57-60; JOHN 19:38 _____

32. Who came with Joseph?

JOHN 19:39 _____

33. How long had Jesus predicted He would be in "the heart of the earth"?

MATTHEW 12:40 _____

34. What statement of Jesus had made a deeper impression on some of His enemies than on His disciples?

MATTHEW 27:63 _____

35. How completely was every loophole plugged, lest His body be stolen, or some trick played?

MATTHEW 27:64-66 _____

Chapter 28 is the Resurrection Chapter

36. On what day did Jesus begin to manifest Himself in resurrection?

MATTHEW 28:1 _____

37. Who were the first witnesses, as it were, of completed redemption?

MATTHEW 28:1 _____

38. What did these women come for?

MATTHEW 28:1 _____

Evidently they too had failed to be impressed with Jesus' prophecy of His resurrection.

39. Who rolled the stone from the door of the sepulchre?

MATTHEW 28:2 _____

40. What effect did the angel's appearance have on the keepers (the "watch," 27:65)?

MATTHEW 28:4 _____

Soldiers set to prevent the Lord's body from being taken from the tomb were paralyzed with fear. God laughs at man's vain efforts to prevent the fulfillment of His Word.

41. What is the epitaph for Jesus' tomb (eleven words)?

MATTHEW 28:6 _____

_____

42. Was it merely the spirit of Jesus that had been raised, or His actual body?

MATTHEW 28:6; LUKE 24:39 _____

43. Of what did the angel remind the women?

MATTHEW 28:6 _____

44. Were angels or humans to carry the resurrection message?

MATTHEW 28:7 _____

This is for the redeemed to do. Saved men and women are the best witnesses of His salvation.

45. Who in particular was to be told?

MARK 16:7 _____

46. As they went to tell the disciples, what two emotions filled these women?

MATTHEW 28:8 _____

47. What word indicates they hurried with the message?

MATTHEW 28:8 _____

48. When Jesus Himself met the women, what did they do?

MATTHEW 28:9 _____

49. What distressing emotion should the knowledge of Christ's resurrection remove from us all?

MATTHEW 28:10 _____

50. What did Jesus now call His disciples for the first time?

MATTHEW 28:10; HEBREWS 2:11 _____

51. Did the watch, or keepers, tell the chief priests facts or fiction?

MATTHEW 28:11 _____

52. Did the chief priests and elders bribe the keepers to circulate facts or fiction?

MATTHEW 28:12, 13 _____

53. Did the keepers agree or refuse to circulate this ridiculous lie?

MATTHEW 28:13-15 _____

54. Where did Jesus say His disciples would see Him?

MATTHEW 28:10, 16 _____

55. What was the reaction of some of the eleven disciples when they saw Him?

MATTHEW 28:17 _____

56. Does any doubt seem to have remained among them a short time later?

ACTS 4:32, 33 _____

57. How much of the human race did Jesus say was to be taught the gospel?

MATTHEW 28:19 _____

58. Converts were to be baptized in whose name?

MATTHEW 28:19 _____

59. What were converts to be taught?

MATTHEW 28:20 _____

60. What promise did Jesus make to those who obey this commission?

MATTHEW 28:20 _____

You have now completed your study of the book of Matthew, and in particular of chapters 27 and 28 on the Triumph of the King. Review as formerly, checking each answer and if necessary the Scripture given. Then take the following test to see how well you understand and remember the truths covered.

In the right-hand margin write "True" or "False" after each of the following statements.

1. At the Jewish trial Jesus was charged with blasphemy. _____

2. Herod thought Jesus was worthy of death. _____

3. Jesus was offered vinegar and gall to dull the pain of crucifixion. _____

4. Jesus was forsaken by God because on the cross He was made to be sin for us. _____

5. The soldiers who crucified Jesus said that He was indeed the Son of David. _____

6. Jesus' prediction of His own resurrection made a profound impression on His disciples. _____

7. The first witnesses of completed redemption were two women. _____

8. The angel reminded the women that Jesus had said He must die. _____

9. The knowledge of Christ's resurrection should remove our fear. _____

10. Jesus said His disciples would see Him in Jerusalem. _____

Turn to page 96 and check your answers.

Suggestions for class use

1. The class teacher may wish to tear this page from each workbook as the answer key is on the reverse side.

2. The teacher should study the lesson first, filling in the blanks in the workbook. He should be prepared to give help to the class on some of the harder places in the lesson. He should also take the self-check tests himself, check his answers with the answer key and look up any question answered incorrectly.

3. Class sessions can be supplemented by the teacher's giving a talk or leading a discussion on the subject to be studied. The class could then fill in the workbook together as a group, in teams, or individually. If so desired by the teacher, however, this could be done at home. The self-check tests can be done as homework by the class.

4. The self-check tests can be corrected at the beginning of each class session. A brief discussion of the answers can serve as review for the previous lesson.

5. The teacher should motivate and encourage his students. Some public recognition might well be given to class members who successfully complete this course.

answer key

to self-check tests

Be sure to look up any questions you answered incorrectly.

A gives the correct *answer*.

R *refers* you back to the number of the question in the lesson itself, where the correct answer is to be found.

In each case, the test number and the lesson number are the same.

Question	TEST 1 A	TEST 1 R	TEST 2 A	TEST 2 R	TEST 3 A	TEST 3 R	TEST 4 A	TEST 4 R	TEST 5 A	TEST 5 R	TEST 6 A	TEST 6 R
1	T	1	F	2	T	1	T	1	T	3	T	2
2	T	4	F	8	F	9	F	3	F	4	T	5
3	F	8	T	10	T	16	F	5	F	10	F	11
4	F	10	T	11	T	24	T	12	T	15	T	14
5	T	12	F	16	F	37	F	20	F	19	F	18
6	F	16	F	20	T	39	T	22	F	20	F	21
7	T	18	F	25	T	47	F	27	F	21	T	23
8	T	20	T	26	F	53	F	30	T	24	T	28
9	F	25	F	30	T	57	T	39	T	29	F	30
10	T	31	T	39	F	65	T	42	F	34	T	42

Question	TEST 7 A	TEST 7 R	TEST 8 A	TEST 8 R	TEST 9 A	TEST 9 R	TEST 10 A	TEST 10 R	TEST 11 A	TEST 11 R	TEST 12 A	TEST 12 R
1	F	1	T	2	F	3	F	2	F	1	T	1
2	T	6	F	6	F	8	T	5	F	6	F	7
3	F	12	T	10	F	12	T	12	T	13	T	18
4	F	14	T	16	T	13	F	18	F	21	T	25
5	T	15	T	21	T	20	F	19	T	25	F	30
6	F	18	F	23	F	23	T	28	T	27	F	34
7	T	22	F	30	T	26	T	32	F	34	T	37
8	F	27	T	32	F	27	F	36	F	45	F	43
9	F	28	F	40	T	38	F	50	T	49	T	49
10	T	43	T	45	T	45	T	62	T	55	F	54

how well did you do?

0-1 wrong answers—excellent work

2-3 wrong answers—review errors carefully

4 or more wrong answers—restudy the lesson before going on to the next one